SCHOOL UNIFORMS, YES OR NO

Bonnie Carole

Rourke
Educational Media

rourkeeducationalmedia.com

Scan for Related Titles
and Teacher Resources

Before & After Reading Activities

Level: **J**   Word Count: **389 words**

100th word: *or* page 7

Teaching Focus:
Concepts of Print: Ending Punctuation- Have students locate the ending punctuation for sentences in the book. Count how many times a period, question mark, or exclamation point is used. Which one is used the most? What is the purpose for each ending punctuation mark? Practice reading these sentences with appropriate expression.

Before Reading:

Building Academic Vocabulary and Background Knowledge
Before reading a book, it is important to set the stage for your child or students by using pre-reading strategies. This will help them develop their vocabulary, increase their reading comprehension, and make connections across the curriculum.

1. *Read the title and look at the cover. Let's make predictions about what this book will be about.*
2. *Take a picture walk by talking about the pictures/photographs in the book. Implant the vocabulary as you take the picture walk. Be sure to talk about the text features such as headings, Table of Contents, glossary, bolded words, captions, charts/diagrams, or Index.*
3. Have students read the first page of text with you then have students read the remaining text.
4. *Strategy Talk – use to assist students while reading.*
   - *Get your mouth ready*
   - *Look at the picture*
   - *Think…does it make sense*
   - *Think…does it look right*
   - *Think…does it sound right*
   - *Chunk it – by looking for a part you know*
5. *Read it again.*
6. *After reading the book complete the activities below.*

Content Area Vocabulary
Use glossary words in a sentence.
agree
arguments
autonomy
conformity
disagree
issue
opponents
proponents

After Reading:

Comprehension and Extension Activity
After reading the book, work on the following questions with your child or students in order to check their level of reading comprehension and content mastery.

1. *Explain how school uniforms affect your decision-making skills?* (Summarize)
2. *What are your thoughts on school uniforms?* (Text to self connection)
3. *Why would regular clothing distract students?* (Asking questions)
4. *What are ways you can share your opinion?* (Summarize)

Extension Activity
Think about what jobs require uniforms. Why do they require uniforms? Would the jobs be just as impactful without the uniform? Think of 3 arguments for and 3 arguments against uniforms in the workplace. After your research, state your opinion and why you came to that conclusion.

Table of Contents

Introduction

I don't like it!

I do!

What is an opinion? Everyone has one. If you ask your friends or family about any topic, how they feel about it is their opinion.

*Others will **agree** or **disagree** with your opinion. We must respect each other's opinions even if they are different.*

Let's talk about school uniforms. Have you thought of the positives and negatives of having school uniforms? Some people like them. Some people don't. But each side has **arguments** that support their opinion.

Arguments for School Uniforms

People who agree school uniforms should be worn are **proponents** of the **issue**. They think school uniforms benefit students, families, and education.

Have you ever been on a field trip where a student wandered off? Or maybe you couldn't easily find your class? School uniforms can help students stay safe on field trips. If everyone looks the same, the group can be easier to keep track of.

Uniforms can make students easy to recognize on campus and off campus. They can make the school a safer place.

Schools have a lot of distractions. Think about what distracts you in school. By having school uniforms, students may be less distracted by what others are wearing.

School uniforms can help reduce bullying. Every student can fit in because they are all wearing the same thing.

Mornings are tough! Uniforms make it easier to get ready for school. Having only one option reduces the stress of choosing an outfit. This can help you make it to school on time.

School uniforms can save money. Families only need to worry about one simple outfit each school day.

School uniforms can create school pride and unity. All students can feel like they are part of the same community because they are all wearing the uniform.

Arguments against School Uniforms

People who disagree with school uniforms are **opponents** of the issue. They see problems with schools requiring students to wear uniforms.

Would you want to look like everyone else each day? Wearing uniforms can promote **conformity**. If all students dress alike, will they start thinking alike?

Opponents say students do not like school uniforms. Not all students like the color or type of school uniform they have to wear.

Choosing an outfit for school gives you **autonomy**. School uniforms can affect your decision-making skills by not allowing you to pick out your clothes each morning.

Students may not learn how to make appropriate clothing choices if the choice is already made for them.

School uniforms have been blamed for behavior problems. Some students make poor decisions and opponents believe it is because they are not allowed to make simple choices such as the clothing they wear to school.

What kind of clothes do you like to wear? What do your clothes say about you? Your clothes allow you freedom of expression. You make choices based on what you like.

Clothes represent what we like and who we are. Shirts that support sports teams, causes, or a band express our interests to the world.

What happens after school? What do you wear then? School uniforms can be an added cost for families. Parents must buy regular clothes and school uniforms.

If you wear uniforms to school you still need to have regular clothes when you get home and on the weekends.

You Decide

Did your opinion on school uniforms stay the same or change? Can you think of more arguments for your side? People share their opinions by writing articles for newspapers or online sources. Share your opinion by writing an opinion paper!

Writing Tips

Tell your opinion first. Use phrases such as:
- *I like* _____.
- *I think* _____.
- _____ *is the best* _____.

Give many reasons to support your opinion. Use facts instead of stating your feelings.

Use the words *and, because,* and *also* to connect your opinion to your reasons.

Explain your facts by using phrases, such as *for example,* or *such as*.

Compare your opinion to a different opinion. Then point out reasons your opinion is better. You can use phrases such as:
- *Some people think,* _____ *but I disagree because* _____.
- _____ *is better than* _____ *because* _____.

Give examples of the positive outcomes of someone agreeing with your opinion. For example, you can use the phrase: *If* _____ *then* _____.

Include a short story about your own experiences with the topic. For example, if you are persuading someone that the best pet is a dog, you can talk about your pet dog.

Restate your opinion so your reader remembers how you feel.

Glossary

agree (uh-gree): to share the same opinion

arguments (ahr-gyuh-muhnts): reasons that support an opinion or idea

autonomy (aw-tah-nuh-mee): being independent or free to choose

conformity (kuhn-for-mi-tee): to think or behave in the same way as everyone else

disagree (dis-uh-gree): to have a different opinion

issue (ish-oo): main topic for debate or decision

opponents (uh-POH-nuhnts): people who are against something

proponents (pruh-POH-nuhnts): people who are for something

Index

Show What You Know

1. What is the difference between a proponent and opponent?
2. Do you think school uniforms promote unity or conformity?
3. Why are arguments important when sharing your opinion?

Websites to Visit

www.readwritethink.org/files/resources/interactives/essaymap

www.grammarly.com/?gclid=CN-m09SuyqwCFcjb4Aodvw5ArQ

www.funenglishgames.com/writinggames/debate.html

About the Author

Bonnie Carole would like to wear a uniform each day! She thinks it would save time each morning and she wouldn't have to think about what to wear every day. As much as she loves fashion, in her opinion, uniforms are a great choice.

Meet The Author!
www.meetREMauthors.com

www.rourkeeducationalmedia.com

PHOTO CREDITS: Cover (left): ©Stocky Images; cover (right): ©Sam74100; title page: ©Blend Images; page 4: ©Syda Productions; page 5: ©Richtt Legg; page 6: ©Steve Debenport; page 7, page 17: ©IS_ImageSource; page 8: ©pixdeluxe; page 9: ©Randy Plett; page 9 (bottom), page 11 (bottom), page 15 (bottom), page 17 (bottom): ©rangepuppies; page 10: ©Piotr Marcinski; page 11: ©JLBarranco; page 12: ©Heidi van der Westhuizen; page 13: ©Giovani Gagliardi; page 14: ©sturdi; page 15: ©Olgatarnik; page 16: ©Kzenon; page 18 (left): ©Ovidiu Hrubaru; page 18 (right): ©Alefotopv; page 19: ©Dmitry Kalinovsky; page 20: ©Dolgachov; page 21: ©Urfin

Edited by: Keli Sipperley
Cover and Interior design by: Rhea Magaro

Library of Congress PCN Data

School Uniforms, Yes or No / Bonnie Carole
(Seeing Both Sides)
ISBN (hard cover)(alk. paper) 978-1-63430-348-4
ISBN (soft cover) 978-1-63430-448-1
ISBN (e-Book) 978-1-63430-547-1
Library of Congress Control Number: 2015931677

Printed in the United States of America, North Mankato, Minnesota

Also Available as:

ROURKE'S
e-Books